X-TREME FACTS: ANCIENT HISTORY

ANCIENT EGYPT

by Catherine C. Finan

BEARPORT PUBLISHING

Minneapolis, Minnesota

Credits:
Title page, 7 bottom left, 10 right, agsaz/Shutterstock.com; 4 top left, Olaf Tausch/Creative Commons; 4 top, Marcella Miriello/Shutterstock; 4 bottom, mariesacha/Shutterstock; 5 top, Nebojsa Markovic/Shutterstock; 5 top left, British Museum free image service/Public Domain; 5 middle, Kokhanchikov/Shutterstock; 5 bottom, akimov konstantin/Shutterstock.com; 5 bottom left, Kiselev Andrey Valerevich/Shutterstock; 5 bottom right, conrado/Shutterstock; 6 top, Harvepino/Shutterstock; 6 bottom, Gerhard Delport/Shutterstock; 6 left, Oliver Denker/Shutterstock; 7 top, David Roberts/Public Domain; 7 top left, ego technique/Creative Commons; 7 top right, Iakov Filimonov/Shutterstock; 7 middle, Jon Bodsworth/Creative Commons; 7 bottom, 10 bottom Unholy Vault Designs/Shutterstock; 7 bottom right, Rhys Davenport/Creative Commons; 8 top, Heinrich Faust/Shutterstock; 8 left, Steve F-E-Cameron/Creative Commons; 8 right, Rombeard/Shutterstock; 9 top, Anton_Ivanov/Shutterstock; 9 top right, LightField Studios/Shutterstock; 9 middle, Olaf Tausch/Creative Commons; 9 bottom, Unholy Vault Designs/Shutterstock; 9 bottom right, Rama/Creative Commons; 10 top, Science Museum, London. Attribution 4.0 International (CC BY 4.0); 10 left, Catmando/Shutterstock; 10 bottom left, Love Lego/Shutterstock; 11 top, Speedster/Creative Commons; 11 bottom, Robiehn/Shutterstock; 11 bottom left, Lawrence Alma-Tadema/Public Domain; 11 bottom middle, Merlin74/Shutterstock; 11 bottom right, Metropolitan Museum of Art/Funds from various donors, 1886/Public Domain; 12 top, Hunefer/Public Domain; 12 bottom,Joshua Avramson 13 top, British Museum/Public Domain; 13 bottom, Elenarts/Shutterstock; 13 top bottom, Nathan B Dappen/Shutterstock; 13 bottom left, Joe Prachatree/Shutterstock; 13 middle, Satinandsilk/Creative Commons; 13 top left, 13 bottom right, Warpaint/Shutterstock; 14 top, azadjain1/Shutterstock.com; 14 left, Scan by NYPL/Public Domain; 15 top, Olaf Tausch/Creative Commons; 15 top left, Codex/Creative Commons; 15 bottom bkgd, 19 top, Yezepchyk Oleksandr/Shutterstock; 15 bottom, Jeff Dahl/Creative Commons; 15 lower bottom left, Kamonrat/Shutterstock; 15 lower bottom right, Ermolaev Alexander/Shutterstock; 16 top, Taranis-iuppiter/Creative Commons; 16 bottom, 18 bottom right, Ernest Board, Attribution 4.0 International (CC BY 4.0); 16 middle, CL-Medien/Shutterstock; 17 top, MusikAnimal/Creative Commons; 17 top middle, Paul Michael Hughes/Shutterstock; 17 middle, Merlin74/Shutterstock.com; 17 bottom, Graficam Ahmed Saeed/Shutterstock; 17 bottom left, Andrey Arkusha/Shutterstock; 17 bottom right, mareandmare/Shutterstock; 18 Olena Brodetska/Shutterstock; 18 bottom left, Belovodchenko Anton/Shutterstock; 19 top left, right, 21 bottom, Albert Kretschmer, painters and costumer to the Royal Court Theatre, Berin, and Dr. Carl Rohrbach/Public Domain; 19 top center, 25 bottom middle bottom, Siren-Com/Creative Commons; 19 bottom, Bist/Shutterstock;19 bottom left, snova.mir/Shutterstock; 19 bottom right, Oliver Denker/Shutterstock; 20 top, Djehouty/Creative Commons; 20–21 bottom, Sir George Touche, 1921/Public Domain; 21 top, Ritagli di Viaggio/Shutterstock; 21 top left, Olaf Tausch/Shutterstock; 22 left, Dorindavidaurel/Creative Commons; 22 right, Kues/Shutterstock; 23 top, Nick Brundle/Shutterstock.com; 23 top right, P. Mullins/Shutterstock; 23 bottom, The New York Times/Public Domain; 24 top, Tawfik Deifalla/Shutterstock; 24 bottom left, Creativa Images/Shutterstock; 24 bottom left, LightField Studios/Shutterstock; 25 top, Krikkiat/Shutterstock; 25 middle, Thesupermat/Creative Commons; 25 bottom, Ttatty/Shutterstock.com; 25 bottom left, paffy/Shutterstock; 25 bottom middle top, Thesupermat/Creative Commons; 26 top, Oleg Znamenskiy/Shutterstock; 26 top left, 26 top right, Ihor Bondarenko/Shutterstock; 26 bottom, emka74/Shutterstock; 27 top, Lawrence Alma Tadema/Public Domain; 27 bottom, Everett Collection/Shutterstock; 27 bottom left, licccka/Shutterstock; 27 bottom right, Keith Schengili-Roberts/Creative Commons; 28 top left, 28 left middle, Marco Ossino/Shutterstock; 28 left bottom, Harmony Video Production/Shutterstock.com; 28 top right, Crackerclips/Dreamstime.com; 28 bottom right, PENpics Studio/Shutterstock; 28–29, Austen Photography

President: Jen Jenson
Director of Product Development: Spencer Brinker
Senior Editor: Allison Juda
Associate Editor: Charly Haley
Designer: Colin O'Dea

Developed and produced for Bearport Publishing by BlueAppleWorks Inc.
Managing Editor for BlueAppleWorks: Melissa McClellan
Art Director: T.J. Choleva
Photo Research: Jane Reid

Library of Congress Cataloging-in-Publication Data

Names: Finan, Catherine C., 1972- author.
Title: Ancient Egypt / by Catherine C. Finan.
Description: Minneapolis, Minnesota : Bearport Publishing Company, [2022] | Series: X-treme facts: ancient history | Includes bibliographical references and index.
Identifiers: LCCN 2021001086 (print) | LCCN 2021001087 (ebook) | ISBN 9781636910956 (library binding) | ISBN 9781636911021 (paperback) | ISBN 9781636911090 (ebook)
Subjects: LCSH: Egypt--Civilization--To 332 B.C.--Miscellanea--Juvenile literature.
Classification: LCC DT61 .F45 2022 (print) | LCC DT61 (ebook) | DDC 932/.01--dc23
LC record available at https://lccn.loc.gov/2021001086
LC ebook record available at https://lccn.loc.gov/2021001087

For more information, write to Bearport Publishing, 5357 Penn Avenue South, Minneapolis, MN 55419.
Printed in the United States of America.

Contents

Journey to Ancient Egypt

If you looked around ancient Egypt, what would you see? **Lush** crops growing along a mighty river in the middle of a sandy desert. People hard at work building a huge pyramid. You'd probably even spot a cat or two! How do we know so much about this incredible civilization from long ago? It's all thanks to what was left behind. Let's explore ancient Egypt!

The ancient **Egyptian civilization lasted for 3,000 years!**

Most Egyptian pyramids were built as tombs for ancient rulers and their families.

Cats were **sacred**. When a pet cat died, ancient Egyptians **mourned** by shaving their eyebrows!

Floods along the Nile River created rich soil for growing crops. The river was also used for transportation.

There were more than 700 **hieroglyphics** in ancient Egyptian writing. **That's a lot harder than learning the ABCs!**

If you unwrapped an Egyptian mummy, **its bandages might stretch as far as one mile (1.6 km)!**

Land of the Pharaohs

Who is the first person you should see if you visit ancient Egypt? The pharaoh, of course! Pharaohs were powerful men and women who led armies into battle, ruled as kings and queens, and were treated like gods. They were thought to control acts of nature, such as the Nile floods, that were important for growing crops. On the flip side, if nature didn't cooperate and people went hungry, the pharaoh might be blamed. Talk about pressure!

The first pharaoh, Menes, united Upper and Lower Egypt over 5,000 years ago.

Menes may have died from being **trampled by a hippo!**

Pharaoh Pepy II took the throne at 6 years old—and ruled for 94 years!

The word *pharaoh* means great house, referring to the royal palaces in ancient Egypt.

The pharaoh's crown had a symbol of a cobra goddess who spat flames at enemies. What a fiery temper!

Pharaohs were said to be the earthly version of Horus, the falcon-headed god of the sky.

Famous Pharaohs

Over 3,000 years, ancient Egypt was ruled by a lot of pharaohs—about 170 of them, in fact. You've probably heard of Cleopatra. She is often remembered for her beauty, but it was her smarts that made her such an impressive leader. Hatshepsut is also often considered one of ancient Egypt's greatest pharaohs. And then there was the boy king Tutankhamun, whose tomb was filled with treasure.

Pharaohs often had beards. Even Hatshepsut—a female pharaoh—wore a fake one!

Ramses II built a great temple with four huge statues of himself at the entrance.

King Tut's grandpa, Pharaoh Amenhotep III, built the famous Temple of Luxor.

Akhenaten and his wife Nefertiti changed Egyptian religion from worshipping many gods to just one—the sun god.

Nefertiti may have ruled as pharaoh after her husband's death.

Making a Mummy

If you were an Egyptian pharaoh, your **reign** began by planning a tomb for your dead body—how cheery! Ancient Egyptians took the afterlife very seriously. **Mummification** preserved the body so it could be joined with the soul after death. First, the body was buried in salt to dry it out. Then, most of the organs were removed, and the empty body was left to dry some more. Finally, it was wrapped with many layers of cloth. Presto—a mummy!

A mummy's organs were put into special jars and buried with the body!

The brain was removed through the nose with a hook! It was thought to be useless and was thrown away.

Even after 3,000 years, the mummy of Ramses II gives us a good idea of what he looked like when he was alive!

The Journey of the Dead

Ancient Egyptians had many beliefs about life after death. Being mummified was just the beginning of a dangerous journey. When the dead got to the afterlife, their fates were decided by weighing their hearts against a feather. If a person had been good, their heart would be lighter than the feather and they would be happy in the afterlife. But if it was heavier? Well, that wasn't good news!

Those unworthy of a happy afterlife were eaten by the goddess Ammit. She had a crocodile's head and a hippo's body.

The dead were judged by Osiris, the god of the afterlife.

Osiris had help from 42 judges to decide the fates of the dead.

The dead traveled by boat through the **underworld**, **which was crawling with creepy creatures!**

Thousands of Gods

Whether taking the journey to the afterlife or awaiting the yearly Nile floods, ancient Egyptians believed their gods controlled it all. There were thousands of gods—one for just about anything you could think of!

The most important god was Ra, the sun god. Isis was the goddess of motherhood. Her son, Horus, was god of the sky. Thoth, the god of knowledge, was no birdbrain. But he did have a bird's head!

To set them apart from ordinary people, **Egyptian gods often had mixed human and animal features.**

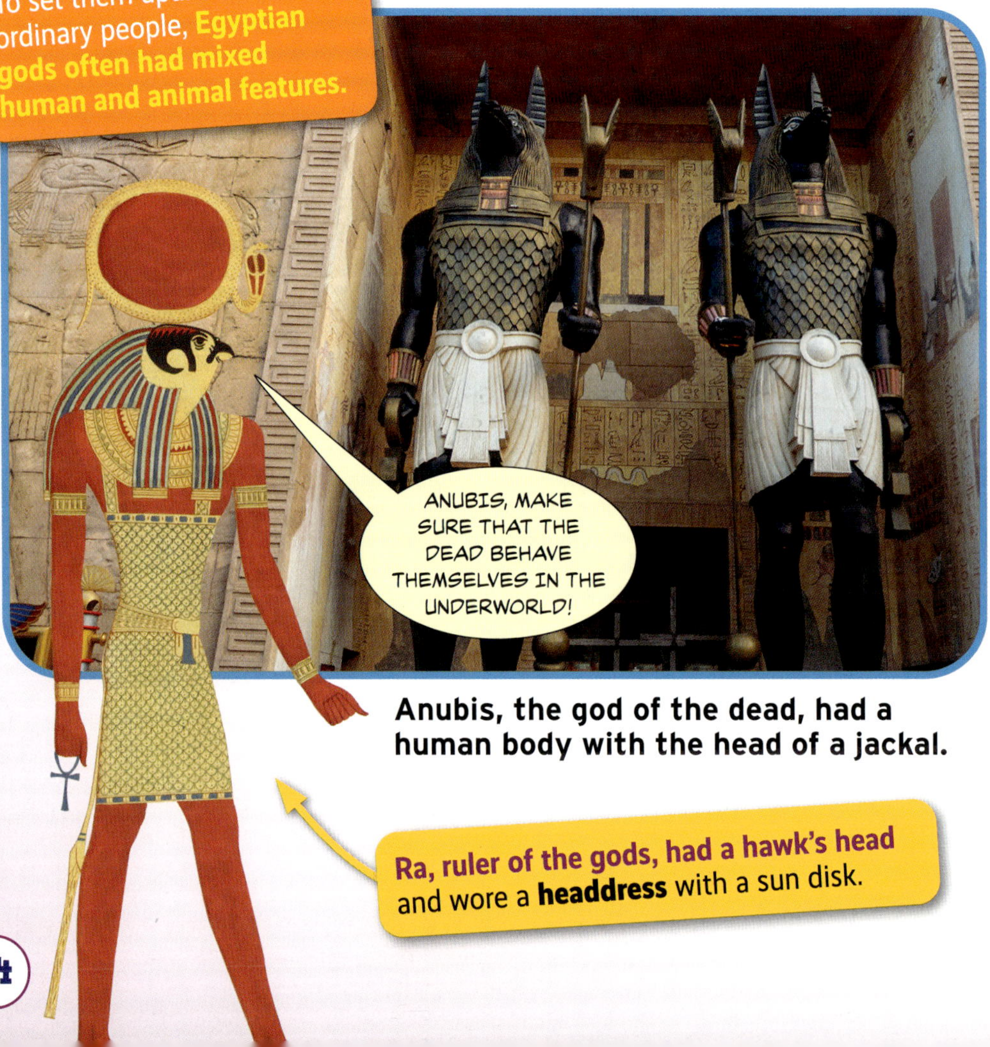

Anubis, the god of the dead, had a human body with the head of a jackal.

Ra, ruler of the gods, had a hawk's head and wore a **headdress** with a sun disk.

Sobek, god of the Nile, had a crocodile's head. Temples built for him contained crocodile mummies!

Totally Terrific Temples

With so many gods in ancient Egypt, there was no shortage of temples for them! Pharaohs ordered some temples to be built for specific gods. Other temples honored dead pharaohs, who were treated like gods. Inside these temples, priests and priestesses performed **rituals** to stay on the gods' good sides and protect Egypt from harm. Ordinary people were kept out. No fair!

The huge temple complex at Karnak honored Ra. More than 80,000 servants, guards, and priests worked there!

Statues of gods at the temples got the royal treatment. Every day, priests oiled them, applied perfume, and offered them real food!

Two huge statues of Ramses II still stand at the entrance of the famous Temple of Luxor.

A long road lined with 1,350 **sphinxes** **once connected the temples of Karnak and Luxor.**

The Temple of Hatshepsut is huge! The powerful female pharaoh wanted her temple to be the biggest and best—and she got her wish!

On the Job

Priests and priestesses working in the temples were highly respected. But it was ordinary Egyptians who really did the hard work to keep life in ancient Egypt running smoothly. Most Egyptians were farmers, craftspeople, traders, soldiers, builders, or **scribes**. Scribes were some of the few people who could read and write—and pharaohs had them write down just about everything. Most of what we know about ancient Egypt is thanks to the scribes!

To stay pure for the gods, **priests bathed many times a day and shaved their heads.**

Egyptians dressed in white **linen** clothes to keep cool. **Both men and women wore makeup and jewelry.**

Doctors used **honey mixed with human brains** to treat eye infections!

The famous scribe Imhotep was also an architect who designed one of the first pyramids. Later, he was worshipped as a god of medicine!

Egyptian bakers used flour that contained grit from the stone tools used to grind wheat. The crunchy bread caused people's teeth to wear away!

Giza's Great Pyramid

Although everyone in ancient Egypt had important jobs, builders did something especially impressive. They created some of the most amazing structures in the world—including the famous pyramids at Giza! To this day, no one knows for sure exactly how these huge structures were built. The largest one, the Great Pyramid, was the tomb of Pharaoh Khufu. The pyramids continue to fascinate people today.

The Great Pyramid was built from more than 2 million stone blocks Each block weighed over 2,000 pounds (907 kg).

The Great Pyramid weighs as much as 16 Empire State Buildings!

Khufu also built pyramids for his three wives, but theirs were much smaller than his. What a guy!

The Great Sphinx statue, carved from rock, sits nearby to guard the pyramids. Its face is probably that of Khafre, Khufu's son.

It took builders 20 years to finish the Great Pyramid.

Farmers helped build the pyramids when flooding kept them from working their fields.

Inside King Tut's Tomb

What's just as famous as the Great Pyramid? The greatest discovery in the history of ancient Egypt—King Tut's tomb! In 1922, **archaeologists** uncovered the tomb of the pharaoh Tutankhamun, better known as King Tut. It was filled with incredible treasures and amazing **artifacts**. Most exciting of all was the pharaoh's mummy, which had been untouched for nearly 3,250 years.

The face of King Tut's mummy was covered with a burial mask made with more than 20 lbs (9 kg) of solid gold.

King Tut died when he was 18. **He might have died because of a broken leg.**

The walls of Tut's burial chamber were painted with scenes of his journey to the afterlife.

Along with statues, jewelry, and other treasures, Tut's tomb contained 48 crates of mummified meat! *Yum!*

King Tut's mummy was inside three coffins. The inner coffin was made of solid gold.

To keep people away from **Tut's** treasure, archaeologists spread the rumor that the **tomb was cursed.**

Those Artsy Egyptians

King Tut's tomb wasn't the only burial place with beautiful artwork on the walls. Most royal tombs had paintings and carvings showing scenes from the rulers' lives and their voyages to the afterlife. Egyptian artists and craftsmen made paintings and statues for tombs. They also made small carvings of things pharaohs may need in the afterlife, such as soldiers, servants, toys, and **utensils**. Even the ancient Egyptians' writing—hieroglyphics—was an amazing form of art!

Hieroglyphics may be Egyptian, but the word is Greek! *Hiero* means holy, and *glyphics* means writings.

Names were written in tombs because people believed that anyone whose name was remembered would live forever!

Art showed pharaohs as much larger than other people. It was good to be pharaoh!

Luckily, many of Egypt's ancient paintings have survived because of the area's dry climate.

Woodworkers placed model boats in tombs to be used in the afterlife.

Artists made beautiful jewelry. Some was buried with the dead to protect them in the afterlife.

Ancient Egypt Lives On

The ancient Egyptian civilization lasted far longer than any other in human history. So, it's not surprising that its impact is still felt today. This incredible culture's well-preserved writing, art, and monuments keep the age of the pharaohs and their people alive—just as they would've wanted it. And some of their inventions are things we still use today! We owe the ancient Egyptians a Great Pyramid-sized thank you!

The ancient Egyptians invented an early kind of paper made from the **papyrus** plant.

The lock and key were invented in ancient Egypt.

What may be the world's oldest bowling alley was discovered near Cairo and dates to around the second century BCE! Strike!

The ancient Egyptians invented toothpaste. It contained ashes, burnt eggshells, and a powder made from ox hooves. *Mmmm . . .* minty fresh!

Want a breath mint instead? Egyptians invented those, too, using cinnamon and honey.

Ancient Egyptians invented eye makeup about 6,000 years ago. They believed it protected their eyes from both infections and the sun.

Black kohl was made from ground minerals and used as an eyeliner. Egyptians believed that **it kept flies away!**

Papyrus Paper

Craft Project

The ancient Egyptians made papyrus—an early kind of paper—using the stem of a plant that grew along the Nile. Two crisscrossing layers of plant strips were soaked in water, hammered flat, and dried into a single sheet. Try making your own papyrus and write like an Egyptian!

Making paper from papyrus plants took many hours of work.

Ancient Egyptian papyrus **scrolls** are displayed in museums all over the world.

What You Will Need

- Scissors
- A paper lunch bag
- A small bowl
- Water
- White glue
- A piece of waxed paper
- A paintbrush
- Pastels

Step One

Use scissors to cut off the bottom of the paper bag. Cut down the side seam and spread the bag open.

Step Two

Tear the bag into strips about ½ inch (1.5 cm) wide. Divide the strips into two equal piles. In a small bowl, prepare a mixture that is one part water and one part white glue.

Step Three

Place the waxed paper on a flat surface. Put one paper strip horizontally along the bottom of the waxed paper. Use a brush to cover the strip with the glue mixture. Place another strip slightly overlapping the edge of the first strip. Cover with glue. Repeat with more strips until the first pile is used up.

Step Four

Repeat step three, gluing the second group of strips onto the first layer vertically (the layers will crisscross). Leave to dry. Carefully peel the paper from the wax paper. Draw on the paper with pastels.

Glossary

archaeologists scientists who learn about ancient times by studying things they dig up, such as old buildings, tools, and pottery

architect a person who designs buildings and manages their construction

artifacts objects from the past that have historical importance

destruction large amounts of damage over a wide area

headdress a covering or decoration for the head

hieroglyphics symbols from the writing system used by ancient Egyptians

linen a type of cloth woven from a plant

lush having a lot of full and healthy growth

mourned felt very sad because someone had died

mummification the process of preparing a dead body for the afterlife by drying it, removing its organs, and wrapping the body in cloth

papyrus a tall plant that grows in water in northern Africa and southern Europe

reign the period of time that a king, queen, emperor, or pharaoh is the ruler of a country

rituals special ceremonies for religious or other purposes

sacred holy or religious

sarcophagus a stone coffin

scribes people who write or copy official documents and manuscripts

scrolls rolls of papyrus used for writing documents

sphinxes mythical figures of ancient Egypt with the body of a lion and the head of a man, a ram, or a hawk

tombs graves, rooms, or buildings designed to house dead bodies

underworld a place where ancient Egyptians believed dead people and spirits lived

utensils simple tools for use in the home and kitchen, such as knives, forks, and spoons

Read More

Flynn, Sarah Wassner. *Ancient Egypt (Weird but True! Know it All)*. Washington, D.C.: National Geographic, 2019.

Hoena, Blake. *The Mummy's Curse: Discovering King Tut's Tomb (Paranormal Mysteries)*. Minneapolis: Bellwether Media, 2020.

Oachs, Emily Rose. *Ancient Egypt (Ancient Civilizations)*. Minneapolis: Bellwether Media, 2020.

Learn More Online

1. Go to **www.factsurfer.com**
2. Enter "**Ancient Egypt**" into the search box.
3. Click on the cover of this book to see a list of websites.

Index

About the Author

Catherine C. Finan is a writer living in northeastern Pennsylvania. She enjoys writing about a wide range of subjects, including ancient history. She hopes one day to see Egypt's Great Pyramid in person!